Weaving without a loo

For Katrina, whose interest in my work from an early age took me back to basics, and so to this book.

Weaving without a loom

Veronica Burningham

SEARCH PRESS

First published in Great Britain 1998

Search Press Limited
Wellwood, North Farm Road,
Tunbridge Wells, Kent TN2 3DR

Text copyright © Veronica Burningham 1998

Photographs by Search Press Studios
Photographs and design copyright © Search Press
Ltd. 1998

ISBN 0 85532 818 5

I would like to give special thanks to my husband,
Mike, for his practical help and moral support
while I wrote this book.

I would also like to thank John Dalton and Sue
Robinson for their help with the diagrams; A. L.
Shuffrey, F.R.P.S. for the photograph of Navajo
weaving on page 7; Val Hayhurst for spending part
of one winter making the belts and bags on page
20; Joe Jackson for lending me his collection of
weaving stick insects on page 21; Shirley Jackson
for making one of the berets on page 41; Geoff and
Brenda Bryon for lending me the three-colour
shawl on pages 54–55, and for giving me much
advice on weaving on hardboard; Jean Tordoff for
allowing me to use her weavings: *Found Objects on
a Beach in Rhodes* on page 61, *Buttertubs Pass* on
page 62 and *The Four Seasons* on page 63.

Thanks are also due to Ann Norman for teaching
me how to make a beret. She and her father, Mr
Richard Blunt, modified some instructions that she
discovered in an old weaving book to produce the
method shown in this book.

Suppliers
If you have any difficulty in obtaining any of
the equipment or materials mentioned in this
book, then please write for further information
to the Publishers:
Search Press Ltd.,
Wellwood, North Farm Road,
Tunbridge Wells, Kent TN2 3DR

Colour separation by P&W Graphics, Singapore
Printed in Spain by Elkar S. Coop. Bilbao 48012

Contents

Introduction

Woven textiles have a history stretching back at least ten thousand years and across every culture. In early textile examples, the majority of fabrics were produced by weft twining, in which two weft threads are twisted together across the width of the fabric, enclosing a warp thread with each twist. Nine thousand weft-twined fabric fragments dating from 2500BC, many elaborately patterned, were recovered at Huaca Prieta, a village on the north coast of modern Peru.

The Australian Aborigines have an unbroken history of at least sixty thousand years, and still use twining extensively for making dilly (carrying) bags, fishing nets and baskets. These are made with handspun string from fibre sources ranging from the cabbage fan palm, eucalyptus bark and pandanus palm, to grasses and hair. The Aborigine women make these bags, and long skinny legs are considered invaluable – legs are used as a 'frame' for the tubular weave!

The Navajo Indians of the American Southwest are famous for their rugs. The rugs are woven with tightly handspun wool on upright looms that are made from little more than wooden poles stuck in the ground. Originally, the Navajo made clothing and blankets but when machine-made goods became available in large quantities, in the 1880s, they were unable to compete and started making rugs for off-reservation markets. Navajo weavers have always enjoyed a high status in society; the ability to weave well is considered to be a gift from the gods. One of their legends suggests that when a baby girl is born, a spider's web that has been woven over the mouth of a hole, should be found and then rubbed on the baby's arm and hand – when the child grows up she will be a weaver, and her hand and arm will not grow tired when she weaves.

Today, technology has taken the drudgery out of routine chores, but our reliance on modern appliances has led us to believe that we cannot try anything new without having the 'right' equipment. Weaving is creative, simple and fun and beautiful things can be produced inexpensively, with virtually no specialised equipment. An expensive loom is not an essential for the weaving process; simple equipment allows freedom to manipulate the threads with your fingers, and you can see exactly how the fabric is produced.

Anyone can weave, and once the basic techniques are mastered, you will be able to make many different items for your home, family and friends. If you want to extend your weaving skills after completing the projects in this book, then is the time to move on to more sophisticated looms.

A Navajo rug being woven on a hand-made loom.

Colour and design

Colours, textures and shapes are all an integral part of the weaving process – you can mix and match yarns and blend and create patterns to produce a never-ending variety of finished designs.

Colour sense

Start building up a scrap book of source materials and yarn wrappings for use as an inspirational reference. Make the yarn wrappings on stiff card. Anchor the yarns to one side of the card with double-sided tape and wind them round the card. Stick another strip of tape across the back of each wrapping and mount them on a page of the scrapbook.

Include individual photographs, postcards and magazine pictures in your scrapbook. Paint a palette of the colours that you can see in each picture and then make yarn wrappings to match the paints (see pages 10–11).

Make collages from scraps of pictures of the same basic colour. Glue the scraps randomly on to a piece of card – you will be amazed at the variety of shades of one colour that you can find. You can then make a small window in a piece of card and move the window over the collage to find a small area that appeals to you. Use the exposed patterns and shades as the basis of a yarn wrapping.

Make wrappings using one type of yarn, with bands of matching or contrasting colours. These are particularly useful when weaving stripes. A very simple but interesting plaid can be created by using bands of three different colours in the warp and two in the weft.

Create wrappings using different types of yarns – shiny, textured or fuzzy for example. Mix them up – shiny yarns peeping through soft fuzzy ones give interesting splashes of colour.

Study a multicoloured, textured yarn and then make a wrapping with bands of other types of yarn in matching colours.

Designing

When designing, bear in mind that warp yarns need to be strong enough to withstand constant manipulation. Smooth cotton or linen make ideal warps. Tightly twisted wool is also suitable, as are many synthetic materials. As a general rule, if the yarn can withstand a strong tug, it is suitable for use as a warp. Fluffy yarns like mohair are not suitable as they tend to stick together, making it difficult to beat the weft into place.

If the warp will show, dark colours give a rich look. Striped warps produce plaid effects and also add depth to the weaving. When the warp is multicoloured, use a plain dark weft to hold it together.

Most materials can be used for the weft, especially if the finished item will not be subjected to constant wear. Adding small amounts of fleece or other natural items such as grasses or sticks can lift a weaving out of the ordinary. Beads, sequins, glitter threads and feathers can all be incorporated to make a special piece. Try cutting up fabric strips or shiny plastic bags and using them to make thick mats.

If you have a precious yarn, lay it in by weaving it under every third or fourth warp thread, and then anchor it in place with a couple of rows of background weft. That way it will stay on top and show to full advantage. Remember that, as with knitting, the texture on knobbly yarns tends to float to the back of the weaving. It may well be that in this case, the back of the weaving will appeal to you more than the front. Twist several thin yarns together to make a weft that will give subtle colour shadings: mix shiny and fuzzy, thick and thin, or smooth and textured.

Try to match yarn colours with the colours in a favourite photograph, postcard or magazine picture. Get into the habit of collecting appealing pictures and build up a file of design sources.

Yarn wrappings
This selection of wrappings is taken from my scrapbook. They were all prepared using the techniques given on page 9.

Basic equipment

Before you start weaving, it is a good idea to gather together the things you will need – they are all readily available and you will probably have most of them around the house. Each project has a list of specific materials and equipment required, but here are some of the most commonly used items.

Card

Card is used to make looms. Get into the habit of saving card from packaging and you will probably find you have the right size and thickness for most of the projects in this book.

Ruler and tape measure

These are used to mark warp spacings on card looms. A ruler will suffice for small projects, but a tape measure is needed for the larger ones.

Pens and pencils

You will need to draw warp and weft patterns on card, hardboard etc., and you can use either pencils or marker pens for this. A pair of compasses is useful for circular designs.

Cutting tools

You will need two pairs of really sharp scissors and a craft knife. Keep your best pair of scissors for cutting yarn and the other for paper and card. A craft knife is better than scissors for cutting straight edges on card.

Needles

A collection of different sizes and types of needle is always useful. Blunt-ended darning needles are particularly good for use with woollen materials. You can also buy flat, blunt-ended bodkins. Some pieces of card can be quite difficult to pierce, so include a thimble in your work box.

Shuttles

These are useful for holding long lengths of weft material during the weaving process. The photograph opposite shows a wooden shuttle which has a tapered edge for beating the weft – you can lay in the weft and beat it down with just one tool. You can also make a shuttle by cutting deep U-shapes in the ends of a small rectangle of stiff card.

Beaters

You will need a beater for beating down the wefts. A simple kitchen fork is suitable for this purpose but dog combs with widely spaced tines are also useful. You may even have a special comb you would like to use, such as the wooden one pictured opposite.

Crochet hook

This is only required for one project (the beret featured on pages 36–41) and is used to reduce the size of the brim to fit.

Wooden dowelling

This is used to stop a warp being wound too tightly. It is also useful to keep the warps away from the surface of card looms, making it easier to lay the weft.

Adhesives and tapes

Masking tape is used to secure dowelling to a card loom, to strengthen the edges of card after the warp is in place, and to make other temporary fixings. Double-sided tape is good for holding yarn windings in place. A glue stick is a useful addition to your work box.

Pliers

These are used to twist wire into circles for mobiles and dream catchers.

Weaving techniques

Weaving is the interlacing of warp ends, the threads that generally run from the top to the bottom of a piece, with weft threads that are woven from side to side. There are many weaving techniques and here I show you some trial weaves using paper. This technique is a quick and inexpensive method of trying out different weaves and colour combinations; it will also help improve your basic skills. Practise the weaves shown on these pages before starting your first project.

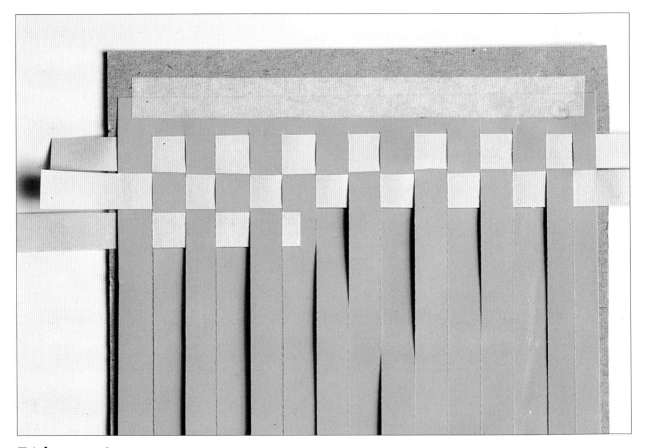

Trial weave using paper
Cut a number of 9mm (³/₈in) slits in a sheet of paper, ending them about 12mm (½in) from the top edge, to create a warp. Cut a contrasting sheet of paper into 9mm (³/₈in) strips for the weft. Secure the warp to a piece of stiff card with masking tape and work the weft strips through the warp. Retain the finished trial weave for future reference.

Tabby weave

This is the basic plain weave, where the weft goes over and under alternate warp threads. The structure is evenly balanced – the warp and weft strips are the same size, and each colour takes up half the space in the weaving.

Prepare a paper warp and some weft strips in contrasting colours. Thread a weft strip under and over alternate strips across the warp. Now weave another weft strip over and under the warps. Repeat these two rows until the trial weave is complete. Try making other samples using different widths of weft strips.

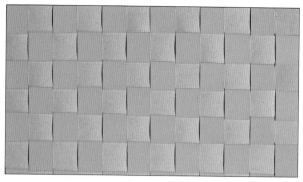

Tabby weave

Twill

Twill is a common weave structure. It involves taking the weft over and under different numbers of warp ends to create diagonal patterns. You need an odd number of warp ends for twill weave structures.

2/2 twill Take the weft alternately under two and over two warp ends to make this version.

3/1 twill In this weave the weft predominates. Take the weft over three and under one warp end. Work the weave in reverse order, over one and under three, to create a 1/3 twill in which the warp is the dominant colour.

2/1 twill Work the weft over two and under one warp end to create this pattern. Reverse the weave, over one and under two, to make a 1/2 twill.

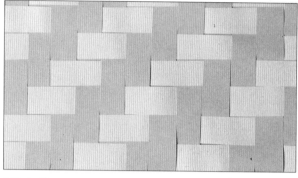

2/2 twill

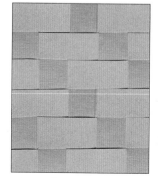

3/1 twill

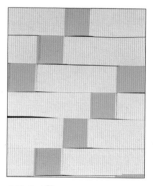

1/3 twill

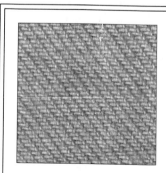

The 2/1 twill is the weave used for the manufacture of denim. The diagonal pattern of the weave is clearly visible in this enlargement of a piece of denim.

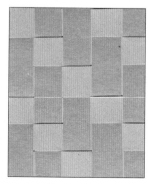

2/1 twill

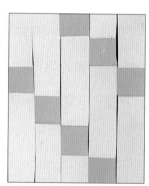

1/2 twill

15

Weaving on sticks

Weaving sticks are used to produce long, thin lengths of fabric which can be made into belts, edgings, trimmings and tie-backs. The fabric produced is a weft-faced weave where the warp ends are entirely covered by the weft.

Two sticks are used to create the simplest weave, but it is more usual to use three, five or seven sticks, depending on the width of the weaving and the size of your hands. In addition to the weaving sticks, you will need warp and weft materials, cotton thread to join the warp ends to the sticks, a small pair of scissors and a darning needle.

Belt

Weaving on sticks is an ideal method to use if you want to make a belt. In this project I show you, step by step, how to do this using five weaving sticks. A wider belt can be made if more sticks are used.

Choose a reasonably strong, smooth yarn for the warp. Cut ten lengths, each four times as long as the finished belt.

You can use any yarn for the weft, but knitting ribbon and fancy textured yarns are particularly suitable.

If you want to be more adventurous, sew the finished strips together to make other items, such as the pretty purse shown on page 20.

You will need

Five 150mm (6in) long
  weaving sticks
Cotton thread
Warp yarn
Weft yarn
Scissors
Large-eyed needle
Button or buckle

1. Attach the warp yarn to the weaving sticks. Tie a small loop of cotton thread through the hole in each stick. Thread two lengths of warp yarn through each cotton loop to make a four-stranded warp end. Gather up all the warp ends and tie them together with a loose overhand knot.

An overhand knot.

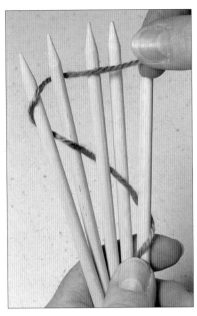

2. Hold the sticks in one hand, and anchor the end of the weft yarn under your thumb. Pass the weft yarn behind and in front of adjacent sticks.

3. Bring the yarn back to the right to complete the figure-of eight movement, then continue weaving up the sticks.

4. Push the weft down and pull it tight when you have woven three or four rows.

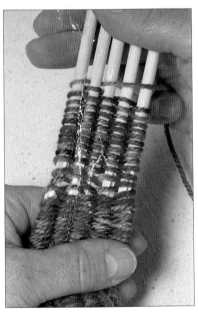

5. When the weft yarn runs short, lay in a new length as shown. Leave the tails in place until the weaving is complete.

6. Continue weaving, keeping an even tension, until the weft nears the top of the sticks.

7. Push the weft down the sticks on to the warp threads. Leave a few rows of weft on the sticks then continue weaving.

8. As the weft lengthens, gradually push it down the warp to the overhand knot. Even out the weft over the whole length of the warp. Remember to leave enough free warp at the other end to tie off.

9. When the weaving is long enough, cut the warp ends away from the cotton loops.

10. Separate each warp end in to pairs of two strands and tie a neat knot in each pair, close up to the end of the weft.

11. For a belt with a buckle and clasp, darn the warp ends back into adjacent warps to make smooth, flush ends to the belt.

12. Alternatively, finish the ends with twisted cords. Twist a knotted pair of warp strands in the same direction as the natural twist of the yarn. Anchor the end and then twist the other pair.

13. Put the twisted ends together and let them both twist back on themselves. Knot the end of each twisted length. Repeat all along the edge.

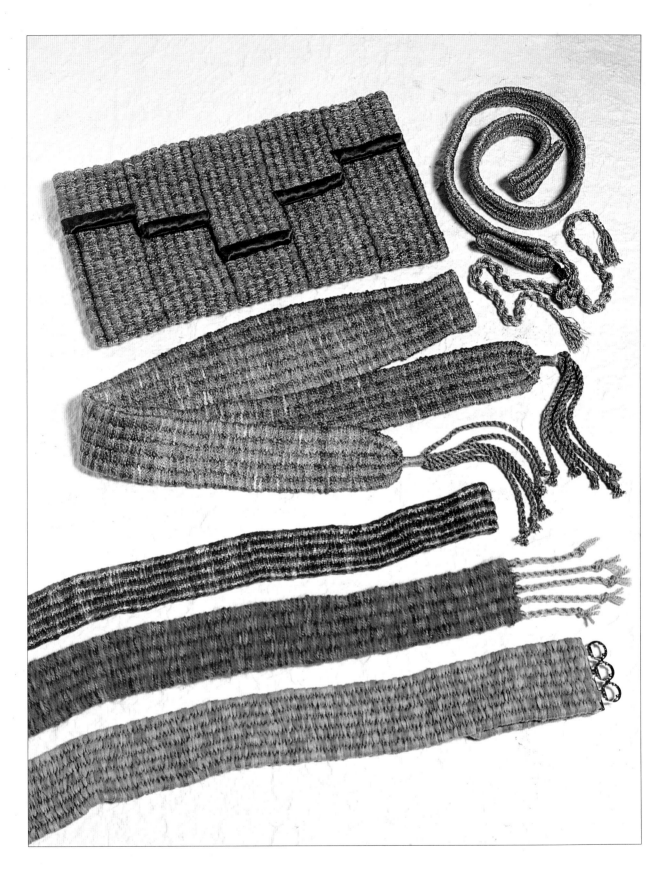

Soft toys

You can also use weaving sticks to make soft toys such as caterpillars, ladybirds and snakes. Use furry yarns and bright colours, add bands of contrasting colours in the weft to make stripes, and embellish the toys with button eyes and embroidered spots.

Opposite

Belts and bags

Stick-woven belts can be finished in various ways: turn back the plain ends of the fabric and then thread a twisted cord through the loops; make extra-long twisted cords and tightly bind them together; darn the warp ends back into the fabric to make a plain end; make twisted cords from the warp ends; or fit a buckle and clasp.

Several lengths of stick-woven fabric can be sewn together to make a bag to match your belt. The plain ends of the fabric used to make this bag are covered with a matching fabric. The same fabric, reinforced with thin card to stiffen the bag, is used for the lining.

Weaving on card

Card is an ideal material for a loom and it is wonderful if you want to experiment with different yarns and colours. It is readily available in various thicknesses, it is inexpensive and it can be used to create a variety of woven items.

For the projects in this chapter, you will need some pieces of card, an old kitchen fork, a selection of bodkins or blunt-ended darning needles, a crochet hook, a pencil and compass, a pair of scissors, a ruler, some wooden dowelling and pipe cleaners.

Table mat

I chose a simple plain weave for this project, where the warp and weft yarns are balanced. I also decided to use two colours, white and turquoise, in both the warp and the weft to create a simple checked pattern. You can alter the look of the finished weave by changing the spacing of the warp and weft, and by varying the thickness of the warp and weft yarns.

Practise cutting equally-spaced slits on scrap card, before starting the project.

For this table mat I use doubled yarn and a 4mm spacing (six threads per inch) for both the warp and weft.

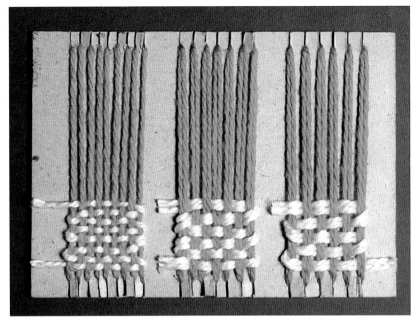

Make small practice weaves using various spacings for the warp and weft and different thicknesses of the yarn.

You will need

Piece of card, 320 x 240mm (12½ x 9½in)

16mm (⅝in) diameter wooden dowelling

Cotton warp yarn

Cotton weft yarn.

Fork

Darning needle

Bodkin

Pencil

Ruler

Scissors

Masking tape

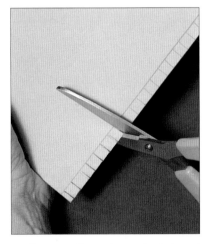

1. Draw a line 6mm (¼in) from each of the short edges of the card. Draw fifty-four short lines 4mm apart (six lines per inch), and then use scissors to cut slits into each end of the card.

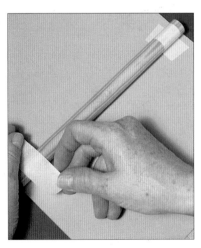

2. Secure a piece of dowelling across the middle of the card with masking tape. This will help ensure that the warp yarn is not pulled too tight.

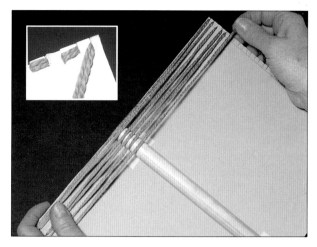

3. Pass the end of the turquoise warp yarn through the first slit at the top of the card. Secure it firmly to the back of the card with masking tape.

4. Take the yarn down the front of the card, through the first slit at the bottom, round through the second slit and up the front to the second slit at the top. Continue winding the warp through the slits until you have six ends. Cut the yarn and secure it to the back of the card with masking tape.

5. Repeat steps 3 and 4 with white yarn. Continue winding, alternating the bands of colour until all the slits are filled.

6. Thread a manageable length of turquoise weft yarn on to a darning needle. Start at the right-hand side of the card and weave the first weft pick across it, taking the yarn over one warp end and under the next one.

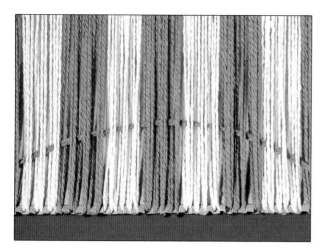

7. Work the weft pick across the warp to create an arc as shown. This will help achieve the correct tension in the weft and prevent the warp pulling in at the sides.

8. Use the fork to beat the first weft pick down to the bottom of the warp. This will avoid unsightly loops of warp yarn at the ends of the table mat when it is removed from the card.

9. Go back to the beginning of the first weft pick and weave the tail end back through three or four warp ends. Leave the excess – this can be cut off when the weaving is complete.

10. Work six weft picks, ending back at the right-hand side. Beat the picks down with the fork to tighten up the weft and create a squared-up pattern. Fix strips of masking tape over the top and bottom ends of the card. This will help stop the warp pulling out of the slits as you work up the card loom.

11. Change to white yarn and start weaving from the left-hand side of the loom. Weave in a new length when the yarn runs short, overlapping the old one through one band of warp colour. Bring the two strands up through adjacent warp threads. Leave the short ends to be trimmed when you have finished weaving. Weave six picks, ending back at the left-hand side.

12. Change back to turquoise yarn and continue weaving from the right-hand side. At the end of the first row, if the white weft yarn is still quite long, take the turquoise yarn round the white before weaving back to the start. This is a neat way of taking the white yarn up the side of the piece ready to start the next set of white weft picks.

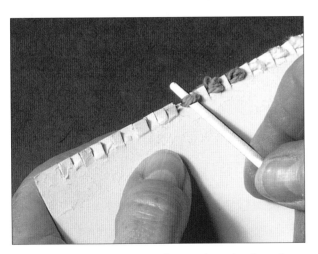

13. Continue weaving, alternating the bands of weft yarn until you reach the top of the card. Carefully remove the masking tape and the dowelling. Use a bodkin to ease the warp off the slits at the top and bottom of the card.

14. Gently work over the piece, adjusting the weave to square up the design, and to fill the warp loops at the top and bottom. Finally, trim off all loose ends.

The finished table mat. See page 28 for variations of this design.

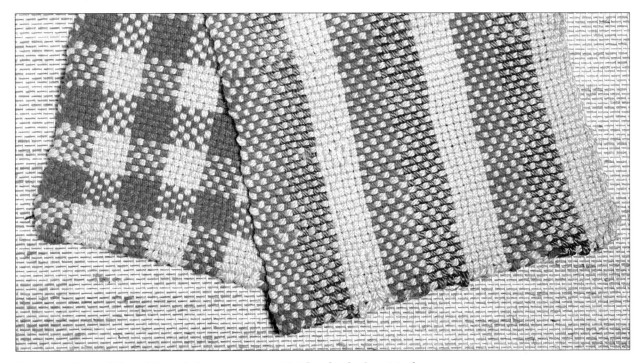

Two variations of the table mat shown on page 27. The checked mat is the same pattern worked in different colours, whilst the striped one has a warp made with alternating bands of red, dark grey and light grey, and a continuous weft of light grey.

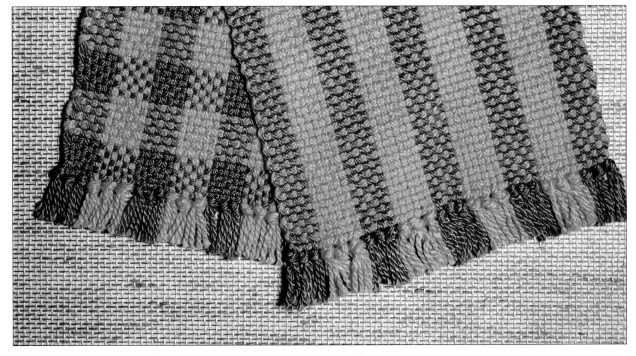

To create fringed ends on table mats you must lay the warp ends as individual cut lengths of yarn. Pass each length through the slits and tape the ends to the back of the card.

Butterfly

When you first start to weave on card you may find it difficult to achieve an even weft tension, and your finished piece may be narrower at one end than at the other. However, this tendency to pull the weft tight can be used to create unusual designs such as the little butterfly below. I used a weft-faced plain weave, with a fine, smooth warp yarn and a weft of soft, variegated mohair, wound with fine glitter yarn.

Prepare the card as shown in steps 1, 3 and 4 on pages 23–24, but omit the dowelling. Cut warp slits at 6mm (¼in) intervals. Draw a line across the centre of the card to ensure that the wings are the same length.

Start the weft at both ends and work into the centre; allow the warp edges to pull in evenly to end up about 75mm (3in) wide. Slip the warp off the card and darn in any loose ends.

Stick a strip of double-sided tape on the card body, fix the end of the weft yarn to the card and then wind the yarn smoothly and closely around the shape. Thread the yarn on to a blunt needle and run it up through the back of the body.

Stitch the body into place. Make the antennae using pipe cleaners wound with weft yarn. Slip them down between the body and wings and secure them with a few stitches.

You will need

Piece of card, 230 x 125mm (9 x 5in)

Small card oval, 75 x 25mm (3 x 1in)

Smooth warp yarn

Weft yarn

Blunt-ended needle

Pipe cleaners

Pencil

Ruler

Double-sided tape

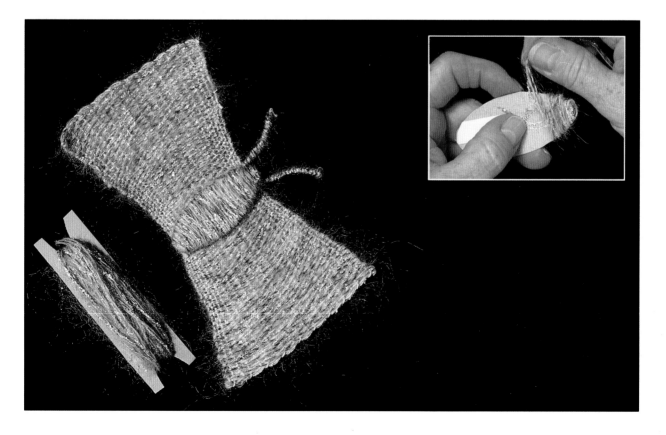

Shoulder bag

This bag will come off the loom all in one piece, with no seams. The warp is wound on both sides of the card, looping round the slits in the top edge of the card only.

Use strong, smooth, non-stretch yarn for practical items such as this. The warp yarn will break if it is too soft, and you will find it hard to beat the weft into place if the warp yarn is too fuzzy.

I chose to use cotton yarn for this bag, white yarn for the warp and white, blue and yellow yarn for the weft.

You will need

Strong card, 300 x 245mm (12 x 9¾in)

Pencil

Pair of compasses

Four 245mm (9¾in) lengths of 10mm (³/₈in) dowelling

Scissors

Cotton warp

Cotton weft

Blunt-ended needle

Comb

Masking tape

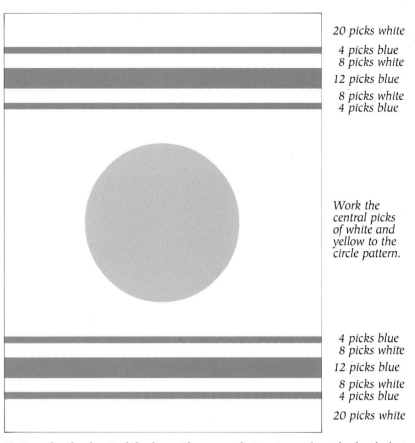

20 picks white
4 picks blue
8 picks white
12 picks blue
8 picks white
4 picks blue

Work the central picks of white and yellow to the circle pattern.

4 picks blue
8 picks white
12 picks blue
8 picks white
4 picks blue
20 picks white

Pattern for the front of the bag. The same design is used on the back, but without the sun motif.

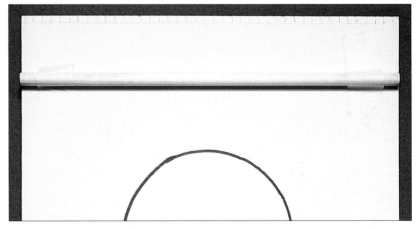

1. Draw a 115mm (4½in) diameter circle for the sun motif on one side of the card. Start 3mm (¹/₈in) from one side and cut thirty-nine slits, 6mm (¼in) apart and 6mm (¼in) deep along the top and bottom edges of the card. Tape two lengths of dowelling to both sides of the card, about 40mm (1½in) from the top and bottom.

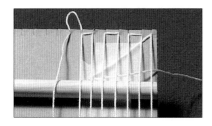

2. Tape the end of the white warp yarn at the top right-hand corner of the back of the card loom. Pass the yarn through the first slit at the top, down the front of the loom, through the first slit at the bottom, up the back and through the first slit at the top again. Take the yarn through the second slit, down the back of the loom, through the second slit at the bottom, up the front and back through the second slit at the top.

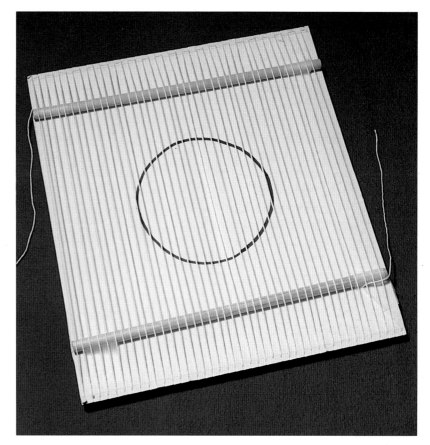

3. Continue winding the warp across the loom. Finish the warp at the bottom right-hand corner of the front of the card. Tape the end of the yarn to the front, leaving a tail. You should have thirty-eight warp ends on the front and thirty-nine on the back.

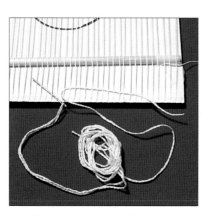

4. Thread white weft yarn on a needle. Start a few warp ends in from the right and weave the weft under and over alternate warp ends.

5. At the end of the row, take the yarn round to the back of the loom and continue weaving through the warp.

6. Weave up to the central motif, changing colours and laying in new threads as necessary (see page 26). Turn the loom upside down and repeat steps 4–6. Weave down to just below the blue bands, finishing somewhere in the middle of the loom.

The dowelling will probably stick out through the sides of the weaving, but when the bag is taken off the loom, the weaving can be adjusted to cover the spaces. If the warp is slack enough, you may wish to remove the dowelling before the weaving starts to cover it.

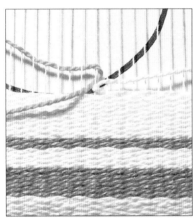

7. Turn the loom round again and start to work the central motif. First, turn the white weft yarn back on itself and lay in a yellow yarn around the same warp end. This link will avoid leaving a hole in the weave.

8. Weave the white yarn across the back of the loom and round on to the front again up to the left-hand side of the sun motif. Turn the white yarn back on itself. Now weave the yellow yarn across the motif and turn it back on itself round the same warp end as the white yarn.

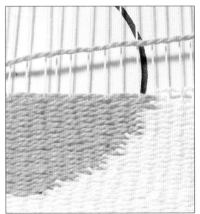

9. Continue weaving with both white and yellow yarns, pick by pick, to build up the central motif and the background. Change the link warp end as necessary to follow the shape of the motif.

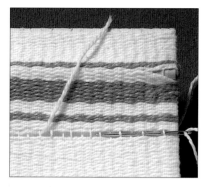

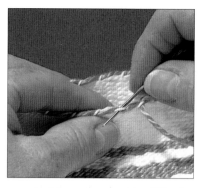

10. When the motif is complete, continue weaving with the white yarn until you reach the weaving at the top of the bag. Weave a final pick to overlap the other tail by a few warps. Trim both yarns. Use the comb to ease the weave from the top and bottom to close the gap.

11. Slip the loops off the top of the card and carefully remove the dowelling from inside the bag. Slide the bag off the loom.

12. Apply a decorative blue finish round the open end of the bag. Thread a length of blue yarn through the warp loops and then work this back on itself.

13. Make two twisted cords for the shoulder strap. Cut two blue and two white lengths of yarn for each cord, twice the length that you want the strap to be. Anchor one end of the white yarns, twist them together in the same direction as the natural twist and then anchor the other end. Twist the two lengths of blue yarn in the same way. Tie one end of the two twisted yarns with a neat knot and anchor this end. Now release the other ends and allow the two yarns to twist back on themselves. Make a second cord in the same way.

14. Sew the cords up the side of the bag; one at the front and one at the back. Twist the two cords together for the length of the shoulder strap, then separate them again and sew the ends down the other side of the bag.

The completed shoulder bag and matching purse.

Purse

Change the loom and the weft pattern slightly and you can make this purse with a flap to match the shoulder bag.

Make a series of marks at 6mm (¼in) intervals along the top and bottom of the card. Start at the left-hand side and cut twenty-three slits across the top and twenty-four across the bottom. Score a line across the card, 90mm (3½in) from the bottom edge. Finally, cut a 3mm (⅛in) slit on the scored line at the right-hand side.

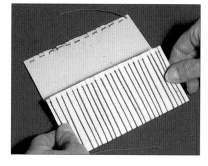

You will need

Thin card, 230 x 144mm (9 x 6in)
Cotton warp yarn
Cotton weft yarn
Pencil
Ruler
Scissors
Blunt-ended needle

1. Start at the top left of the card and wind the blue warp yarn on one side only (see page 24). Finish the long warp ends at the bottom right and then make an extra warp end up to the horizontal slit.

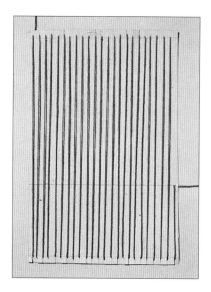

2. Turn the card over and fold it along the score line. Join the sides of the fold with masking tape.

3. Use the weaving method shown on page 31 to work the weft round the front and back of the card starting at the bottom fold. At the top of the bag section, work the weft to and fro to form the flap. Make a single twisted cord from one white and one blue length of yarn and sew it to the purse.

Beret

Weaving does not only have to be restricted to rectangular shapes with horizontal and vertical lines. When you understand the basic techniques, you can have a lot of fun by changing the shape and direction of the warp and/or weft.

In this project I show you how to make a beret by weaving round a circular warp. The warping pattern opposite may appear complicated at first sight, but winding the warp is a simple matter of following the numbers, passing the needle down through the crosses and up through the circles. Enlarge the pattern by 190% and you will be able to make a beret that will fit most heads; the brim can be reduced to size with a crochet hook.

Choose thick, soft wool for both the weft and warp.

You will need
Thin card, 350mm (14in) square
Pencil and compass
Warp yarn
Weft yarn
Scissors
Blunt-ended needle
Crochet hook
Ruler

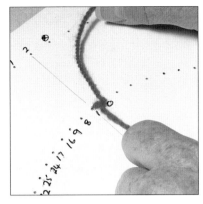

1. Thread a long length of warp wool on to a blunt-ended needle and take it down through hole 0 and up through hole 1. Pull the wool through to leave a tail at hole 0 and tie a loose knot between holes 0 and 1.

2. Take the warp down through hole 2.

3. Take the warp across the back of the card and up through hole 3. Do not pull the warp too tight.

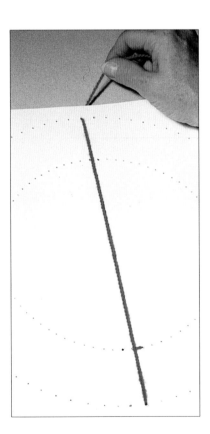

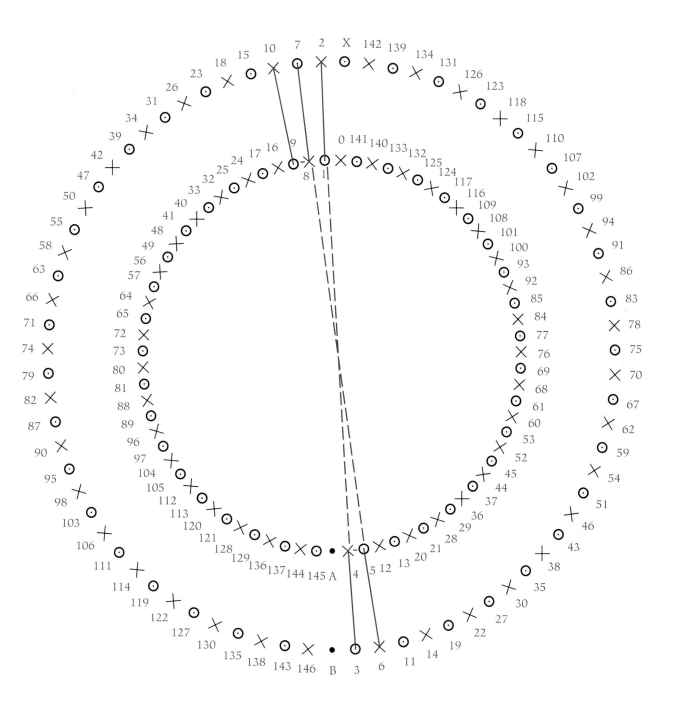

Warping pattern for the beret. Use a photocopier to enlarge it to 190% and the finished beret will fit most heads. Tape the pattern to a piece of thin card and pierce the centre of all the circles and crosses with a needle. The red lines show the first few movements for the warp: the short solid lines are on the front of the card and form the warp ends for the brim of the beret; the broken lines are on the back of the card and form the warp for the top of the beret.

4. Turn the card loom over and take the warp down through hole 4 and up through the adjacent hole 5. Take care not to catch the long warp end (across the back of the loom) under this small loop. Continue threading the warp, taking the wool up, down and across the pattern, following the numbered sequence. Check that you maintain an even tension on both sides of the loom. Join on new lengths of warp with reef knots as shown, leaving 50mm (2in) tails to be woven in when you have finished weaving.

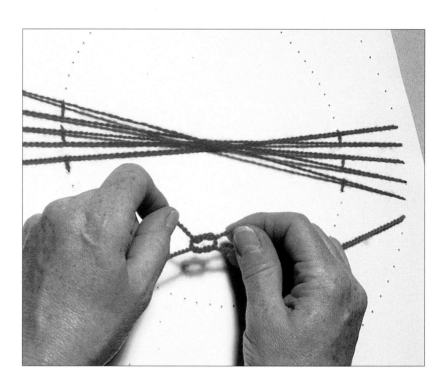

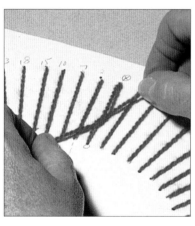

5. Continue threading the warp up to hole 146; take the warp down through this hole, across the back of the loom and up through hole X. Release the knot between holes 0 and 1 and tie a new knot between holes 0 and X. You now have an even number of warp ends, but you need an odd number of ends to complete the warp.

6. Holes A and B are used to create the last warp end and to start the weaving. Thread a long length of wool on the needle and tie it to the short loop on the back of the loom, adjacent to hole A. Take the wool down through hole A and up through hole B.

7. At a point about 12mm (½in) short of the centre of the warp, secure the wool to an adjacent warp end with a half-hitch knot to complete the warp. The remaining length of wool is used to start the weaving.

8. Start weaving from the centre outwards, taking the wool under and over adjacent warp ends. You will find it easier to work round the outer edges of the warp.

9. Pull the wool gently in towards the centre to give a textured effect. Do not pull too tightly.

10. Continue weaving round and round the warp, from the centre outwards. Overlap the ends when joining in new lengths (see page 18). Vary the texture across the top of the beret by increasing and decreasing the number of strands of wool, or by changing to a different weave (see pages 14–15). Finish the outer edge in plain weave.

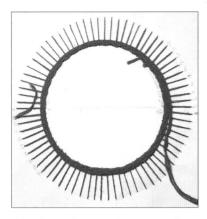

11. Turn the card over and work the brim in plain weave, using either a single or double strand of wool. Work from the inner edge outwards to complete the brim.

12. Carefully remove the card loom from the beret by tearing it away in small sections. If you have to use scissors, take great care not to cut any of the warp ends.

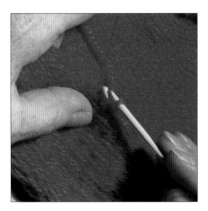

13. Finally, work one or two rows of single crochet round the brim to adjust the size and to provide a neat finish to the edge.

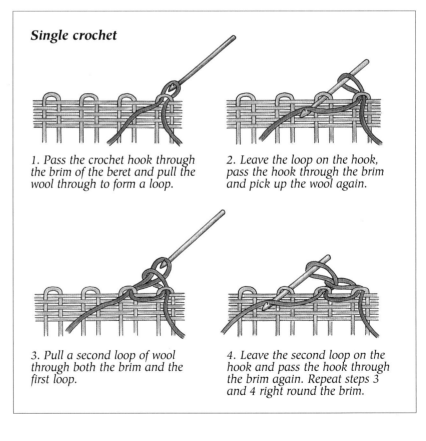

Single crochet

1. Pass the crochet hook through the brim of the beret and pull the wool through to form a loop.

2. Leave the loop on the hook, pass the hook through the brim and pick up the wool again.

3. Pull a second loop of wool through both the brim and the first loop.

4. Leave the second loop on the hook and pass the hook through the brim again. Repeat steps 3 and 4 right round the brim.

Three berets made on card looms – the pink one at the back is the finished project.

Weaving on rings

Rings are fun to weave on and you can use them to make mobiles and dream catchers. Unlike a card loom, they become an integral part of the finished design. The circular frame can be completely covered with yarn, or spaces can be left, depending on the type of effect you want to create.

You will need an embroidery hoop or you could use wire twisted into a ring with a pair of pliers. You will also need warp and weft yarns and items such as beads, buttons, feathers and woollen pompoms to decorate the weaving.

Rings

Wooden embroidery hoops are ideal for this type of work; they have a wide rim that allows you to weave a different design on each side. You can make your own rings using sturdy, plastic-covered wire which is available from DIY stores and some art and craft suppliers. Basket weaving suppliers often stock a variety of rings and hoops. You may also be able to salvage suitable small rings from discarded toys.

Yarns

The best yarns for warping on rings are those with a slightly rough surface – this prevents them from slipping. However, smooth, slippery yarns can be anchored to a ring with strips of double-sided tape. Alternatively, the ring can be completely wrapped with ribbon or yarn and the warp yarn can then be anchored to the covering material. Boucle and fancy yarns are ideal for wrapping rings.

You can decorate mobiles and dream catchers with a variety of materials and objects: coloured feathers, buttons, beads, ribbons and woollen pompoms are just a few suggestions.

Moon and star mobile

Mobiles are easy to make, and fun to do. Here I have used an embroidery hoop as the basic frame. I have chosen a silver glitter yarn for the moon and star, which is worked over dark blue warp threads. This frays easily but the finished effect is well worth the effort!

You will need
Embroidery hoop, 180mm (7in) diameter
Double-sided tape
Ribbon, 1m (1yd) long, 25mm (1in) wide
Cotton warp yarn
Glitter weft yarn
Large-eyed needle
Ruler
Paper
Invisible thread

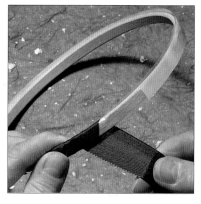

1. Stick a strip of double-sided tape round the outside of the ring. Peel off the backing from the tape and bind the ribbon evenly round the ring.

2. Thread the warp yarn on to a needle and anchor the warp to the ribbon. Start with the long warp ends at the centre of the ring and work outwards – space the warp ends evenly and maintain an even tension.

3. Use glitter weft yarn and a tabby weave for the silvery moon. Work from the top and bottom into the middle of the warp, and allow the weft to pull in slightly to create an even curve.

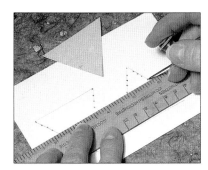

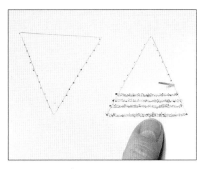

4. Prepare the star. Draw two equilateral triangles side by side on good quality paper. Use a ruler as a guide, and pierce a set of evenly-spaced holes in both triangles as shown.

5. Start at the base of one triangle and wind a warp across the triangle to finish at the apex.

6. Work the weft in tabby weave, from the apex down to the base and up again. Do not pull the warp ends out of alignment. Fill one half of the triangle, thread the yarn back to the middle of the base and fill the other half.

7. Work the other triangle in the same way then carefully pull the paper away from both woven triangles.

8. Place one triangle over the other in a star shape and stitch them together using invisible thread.

10. Hang the star in the open area of the embroidery frame using invisible thread.

Sun mobile

This simple mobile uses two concentric rings. Glitter yarn is used for the warp and weft on the inner ring to represent the sun, and the gap between the two rings is simply wound with gold and orange silk yarn to form sun rays.

You will need

Two embroidery hoops, 230mm (9in) and 75mm (3in) diameter
String
Warp yarn
Weft yarn

1. Centralise the small ring within the large one using lengths of string.

2. Bind the rings together with weft yarn and remove the string ties. Use glitter yarn to warp up both sides of the inner ring (see page 43) and then work both sides using tabby weave.

The finished sun mobile together with the moon and star mobile.

Dream catchers

Native Americans believe that if you hang a dream catcher by your bed, any bad dreams will be caught and burnt up by the heat of the sun the following day. Good dreams will slip through the catcher to be dreamt again. Originally, dream catchers were made from sinew woven into a regular spider's web design, and then decorated with beads and feathers. A dream catcher can be any size – it all depends on the size of your dreams!

The straps that crisscross this dream catcher are woven, one at a time, on warps attached to a wire hoop which is bound with woollen yarn. The background colour is woven up the full length of the strap, leaving gaps in the weft after every eight or ten picks. Two picks of a contrasting weft yarn are then woven in the gaps and looped up one side of the strap and down the other. When one strap is completed, another is warped up across it. Pompoms sewn on to plaited wool tassels provide added decoration.

Opposite
Selection of dream catchers
The dream catcher in the top left is made on a cane ring. The strips are woven on sets of warps wound across the ring and then the yarn is looped round the strips to form the spider's web. The design in the top right uses different yarns of the same colour to give interesting textures. It is woven on a wire ring bound with one of the yarns. A natural wooden hoop is used for the bottom dream catcher. Yarns are knotted together round the ring, from the outside into the centre, to form the web.

Weaving on hardboard

Large weavings, such as the shawl featured in this chapter, need to have a stable loom. Hardboard is ideal for this purpose as it is durable, strong and tough. Most DIY and large hardware stores stock sheets of hardboard and will often cut a piece to the required size. Stiff cardboard can also be used, but it is not nearly as sturdy as hardboard. You will also need a support for the loom, a junior hacksaw to cut slots for the warp, and some warp yarn.

Triangular weaving

You can use hardboard as a loom for weaving large rectangular shapes, but it is also ideal for weaving triangular shapes of fabric such as the shawl featured on pages 50–53.

This type of weaving is a derivation of an ancient craft which is still practised by some tribes in South America. These tribal craftsmen make their looms from branches cut from trees. The branches are smoothed off and then lashed together in a square, with their ends overlapping at the four corners. The weavers warp up the loom and kneel on the ground while working on the fabric.

You can use the method shown on the following pages to prepare trial weavings on small card looms as shown below. Experiment with different thickness of yarn and various colour combinations.

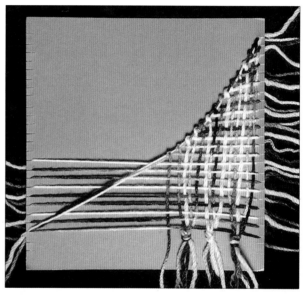
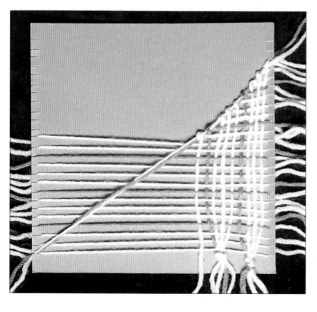
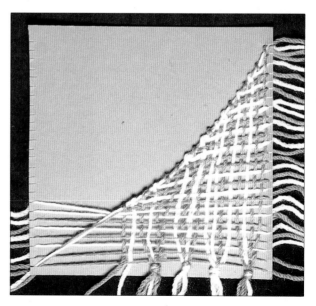

Shawl

In this method of weaving the warp ends become weft picks when they have been knotted to a diagonal cross thread. The weaving is removed from the board as a finished piece.

Soft yarns are best for this type of project – light fuzzy yarns such as mohair are ideal. Fine yarns give an open weave, thicker yarns a closer and heavier weave. Add a fine glitter yarn to each warp end for a more elegant look.

The most important thing to remember when working this triangular method of weaving is to keep the tension very even.

1. Make a series of pencil marks at 6mm (¼in) intervals, down two opposite sides of the hardboard. Use a junior hacksaw to cut 6mm (¼in) deep slits at each mark to take the warp ends.

Now make another series of pencil marks, again at 6mm (¼in) intervals, across the bottom of the board. These will help you maintain a uniform spacing between the weft picks.

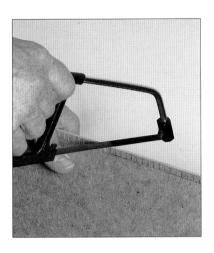

You will need

Piece of hardboard, 1200mm (48in) square

Large-eyed needle or bodkin

Junior hacksaw

Warp yarn

Easel

Pencil

Ruler/tape measure

Scissors

2. Cut strands of yarn 600mm (24in) longer than the width of the board. Cut a length of wool for each pair of slits – you will need an equal number of two contrasting colours. Warp up the loom, leaving 300mm (12in) of each length protruding at both the left- and right-hand sides of the loom.

3. Cut two lengths of wool, one of each colour, 150mm (6in) longer than the warp threads. Stretch them together diagonally across the loom, from the bottom left-hand slot to the top right-hand slot.

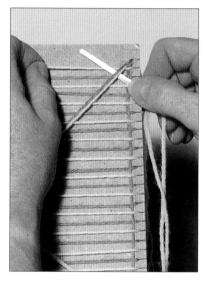

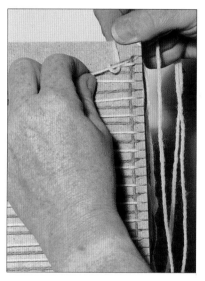

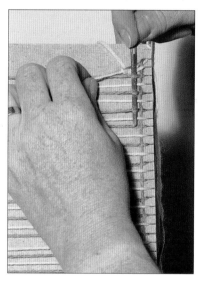

4. Release the left-hand side of each warp end and thread it on to the bodkin. Hold the warp end in one hand, close to the double cross thread, and take the free end of the warp over the double cross thread and back under it as shown.

5. Pull the wool tight to make a half knot, 6mm (¼in) across the board from the previous weft pick.

6. The free end of the warp now becomes the weft. Weave the wool down through the other warp ends to the bottom of the loom, keeping it parallel to the side of the loom.

7. Work down the warp and repeat steps 4–6 with each warp end. The weft picks should align with the pencilled marks across the bottom of the loom. The knots on the double cross thread make a neat edge on the finished shawl.

8. Use the lengths of wool left hanging from the bottom of the loom to form a fringe on one side of the shawl. As you complete every four picks, knot their strands together just below the bottom warp end.

 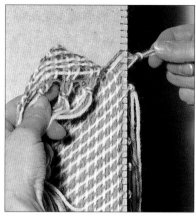

9. When you have finished weaving, knot the strands of wool in the slits at the right-hand side of the loom. Work from the top and tie the strands, again in groups of four, at the back of the loom.

10. When you have finished knotting, gently ease each knotted section out of the slits at the right-hand side to remove the shawl from the loom.

The finished shawl
The woven shawl should be washed in soapy water to set the weave. You should then rinse it thoroughly and lay it flat to dry, making sure the fringe is straight. When the shawl is dry, tidy up the fringe by trimming the ends.

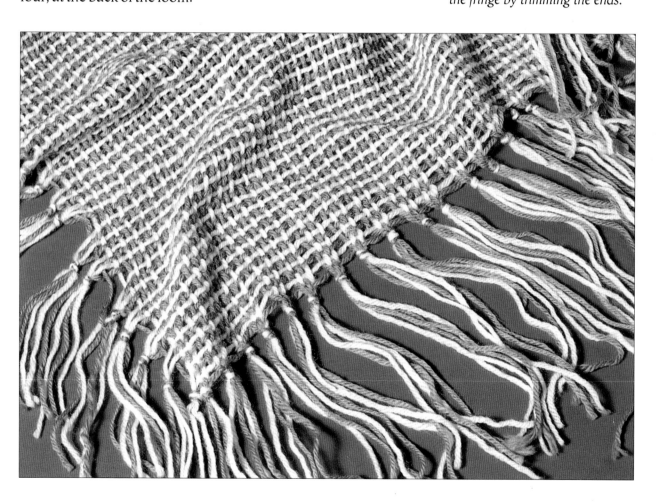

Beautiful shawls can be woven
using the triangular method of
weaving shown on the previous
pages. The shawl at the top of
this picture was woven with a
thick, heavy wool and I used a
finer wool for the shawl on the
left, which gave a more open
weave and softer feel. Handspun
yarn was dyed naturally with
vegetables and used to create the
soft, close-textured shawl on the
right.

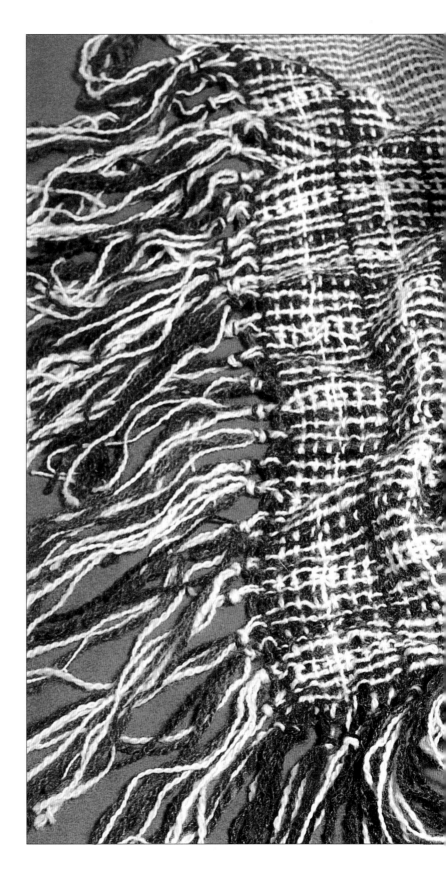

Weaving on picture frames

Picture frames make good looms for small projects, especially for tapestry pictures where the frames become part of the finished weaving. You can often purchase second-hand frames at a reasonable price, but do make sure they are quite sturdy. Reinforce the corners with small angle brackets and smooth any rough edges that might catch the threads.

You will also need a shuttle for the weft yarn, shed sticks made from strips of cardboard, string leashes, strong cotton warp yarn and a selection of weft yarns.

Tapestry

Tapestry is a weft-faced weave – the warp is completely covered by the weft. A shuttle of weft yarn is passed back and forth across the warp in plain weave, through two 'sheds' – the spaces between two sets of warp threads. However, you can also change the texture of a tapestry by manipulating the warp ends by hand, for say a twill weave structure, or by using other techniques such as knotting.

Small scale tapestries allow you to experiment and to try out different ideas. The smaller the project and the finer the yarns, the closer the warp ends should be set.

For this project I use a small frame to make a simple tapestry of a garden scene, where the texture and colour of the yarns paint a picture. I also use a smooth, strong cotton yarn for the warp ends and a variety of yarns for the weft.

You will need

Frame 300 x 375mm (12 x 15in)

Two card shed sticks

Shuttle

String

Warp yarn, approximately 15 metres (15 yards)

Weft yarns

Pencil and ruler

Scissors

Fork

1. Use a pencil to mark the top and bottom of the frame at 12mm (½in) intervals, leaving 25mm (1in) at each side. Tie the warp yarn to the bottom left-hand mark, take it up the front to the first mark at the top and down the back to the second mark at the bottom. Continue winding the warp smoothly and evenly around the frame and then tie it off at the top right-hand corner.

2. Bring the upper and lower set of threads together with a shed stick; insert the stick between every other thread and push it towards the top of the frame to keep the warps taut. Insert the other shed stick under the opposite warp ends.

3. Tie a leash (a small loop of string) round each of the threads in the lower warp. Tie groups of four leashes together. These leashes are used to lift the opposing shed.

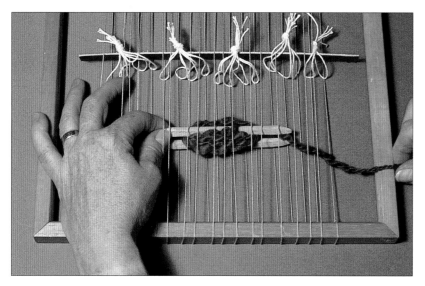

4. Wind a shuttle with the first weft material. Turn the lower shed stick on its side to lift the top shed and pass the shuttle from right to left to make the first row.

5. Turn the shed stick flat and lift groups of leashes to raise the opposing shed and pass the shuttle back to the right. A few rows of tabby, well beaten down, will be sufficient to spread the warp.

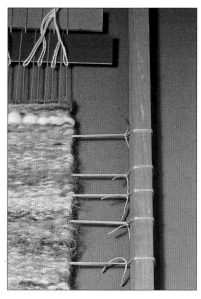

6. Continue weaving, using the shed stick and the leashes to lift the appropriate shed. Change colours by overlapping the yarns across two or three warp ends. Mix the colours in each row using several thinner yarns to add depth and to create gradual changes in colour.

7. As the weaving progresses add leashes to the sides of the frame to maintain an even width.

The finished tapestry. Different colours and textures were used to create the impression of a garden and sky. To remove the tapestry from the frame, small groups of thread were cut and knotted together. These were then taken to the back of the design and secured with stitching.

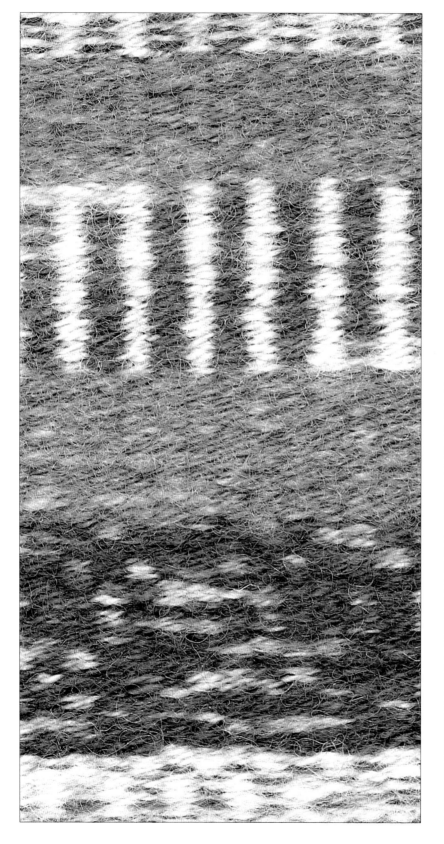

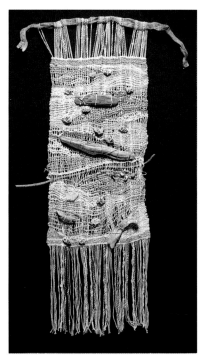

Found Objects on a Beach on Rhodes *by Jean Tordoff*

A warp of knitting cotton was suspended from a dried branch found on a beach near Trianta. Pebbles, shells and pieces of wood and glass were collected from the same place then incorporated in the weaving. Pebbles were enclosed in a net crocheted from fine strong string with long ends that were then woven into the fabric. The weft was woven with lots of space between picks to create the effect of torn fishing nets.

Opposite
Blue landscape
Tie-dyed, handspun wool was used to make this indigo, plain weave wallhanging. The design is loosely based on a viaduct and surrounding moorland near my home in Yorkshire, England.

61

Buttertubs Pass by Jean Tordoff
This landscape tapestry was woven on a home-made frame using a
postcard of the scene as a reference. The warp of fine cotton was wound
round the frame in a similar way to that shown on page 57. The weft
materials include a mixture of tapestry wools and fine knitting wools.
Strands of different shades of wool were mixed together to increase the
range and depth of colour. Surface embroidery was added to the weaving
to enhance definition.

Opposite
The Four Seasons by Jean Tordoff
This tapestry was woven on an old window frame. Hooks were
fitted on the top and bottom edges and the warp was wound round
two lengths of dowelling held under tension by the hooks. The weft
materials were sorted into colour groups and textures. The spring
and winter panels were woven entirely with smooth yarns, whilst
the summer and autumn panels were woven with smooth and
textured yarns, and augmented with textured stitches. The shapes
of the different areas evolved as the weaving progressed.

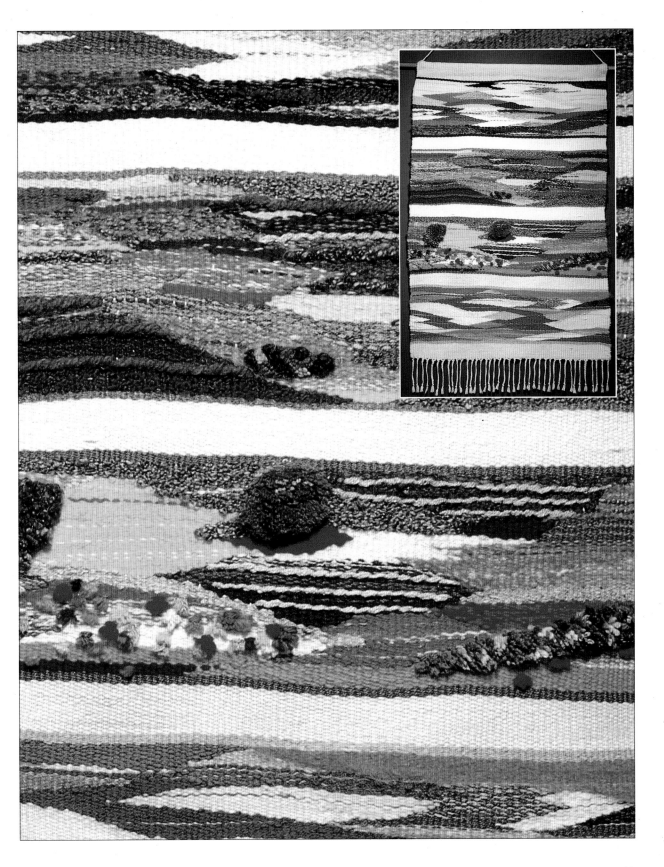

Index